Fun-to-Read Picture Books have been
grouped into three approximate readability
levels by Bernice and Cliff Moon. Yellow
books are suitable for beginners; red books
for readers acquiring first fluency; blue
books for more advanced readers.

This book has been assessed as Stage 5
according to *Individualised Reading*, by
Bernice and Cliff Moon, published by
The Centre for the Teaching of Reading,
University of Reading
School of Education.

First published 1986 by
Walker Books Ltd
184-192 Drummond Street
London NW1 3HP

First printed 1986
Printed and bound by
L.E.G.O., Vicenza, Italy

British Library Cataloguing in Publication Data
West, Colin
'Have you seen the crocodile?' (Fun-to-read
picture books)
1. Title   II. Series
823'.914[J]   PZ7
ISBN 0-7445-0526-7

'Have you seen the crocodile?'

Written and illustrated by
Colin West

WALKER BOOKS
LONDON

'Have you seen the crocodile?' asked the parrot.

'No,'
said the
dragonfly.

'Have you seen the crocodile?'
asked the parrot
and the dragonfly.

'No,'
said the
bumble bee.

'Have you seen the crocodile?'
asked the parrot
and the dragonfly
and the bumble bee.

'No,'
said the
butterfly.

'Have you seen the crocodile?'
asked the parrot
and the dragonfly
and the bumble bee
and the butterfly.

'No,'
said the
hummingbird.

'Have you seen the crocodile?'
asked the parrot
and the dragonfly
and the bumble bee
and the butterfly
and the hummingbird.

'No,' said the frog.

'No one's seen the crocodile!'
said the parrot
and the dragonfly
and the bumble bee
and the butterfly
and the hummingbird
and the frog.

But then...

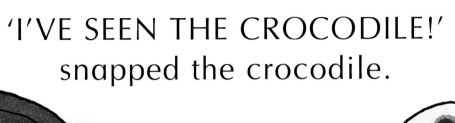

'I'VE SEEN THE CROCODILE!'
snapped the crocodile.

'Have YOU seen the parrot
and the dragonfly
and the bumble bee
and the butterfly
and the hummingbird
and the frog?'

asked the crocodile.